Jewish Neighborhoods in California:
History and Development

Keith Warwick

Jewish Neighborhoods in California: History and Development

Keith Warwick

Academica Press
Washington - London

Library of Congress Cataloging-in-Publication Data

Names: Warwick, Keith, author.
Title: Jewish neighborhoods in California : history and development / Keith Warwick.
Description: Washington : Academica Press, 2020.| Includes bibliographical references. | Summary: "Jewish Neighborhoods in California: History and Development amplifies the essence of Judaism as experienced in California's historic Jewish neighborhoods."-- Provided by publisher.
Identifiers: LCCN 2019045979 | ISBN 9781680532067 (hardcover) | ISBN 9781680532081 (paperback)
Subjects: LCSH: Jewish neighborhoods--California--History.
Classification: LCC F870.J5 W37 2020 | DDC 979.4/004924--dc23
LC record available at https://lccn.loc.gov/2019045979

Copyright 2020 Keith Warwick

Dedication

To my beloved father Benjamin Warwick, April 12, 1932- July 5, 2019.

CONTENTS

Chapter 1 Introduction 1

Chapter 2 Chassidic 11

Chapter 3 San Francisco 15

Chapter 4 Sacramento and Stockton Area 29

Chapter 5 Oakland and the Remainder
of the San Francisco Bay Area 33

Chapter 6 Los Angeles 43

Chapter 7 Long Beach, San Diego the Central Valley 73

Chapter 8 Conclusion 81

Bibliography 83

Index 85

CHAPTER 1
INTRODUCTION

The Torah. The family. The kiddush. The joy. "Jewish Neighborhoods in California: History and Development" amplifies the essence of Judaism. This title contains facts, images, inspiration and a little of what the author calls poetry.

The author's son, Matthew Warwick

The author's son, Evan Warwick

There have been, are, and will always be Jewish neighborhoods in California. Some are historical holding a remnant of the Jewish population that resided there decades or a century ago. Some are new and developing. These range from Oakland's Jewish Community Center in West Oakland to several Jewish enclaves in San Francisco. Los Angeles is a national Center of Judaism.

**Boy Scout gets Jewish Ner Tamid from
Rabbi William Kramer Courtesy of University of California**

If one were only to study neighborhoods that have become extinct it would be sad. If one were only to study neighborhoods that are modern, we would lose the intimacy, romance and passion of studying these historical Jewish communities.

Polish American Jewish Woman (circa 1910)
Courtesy of California State Library

A Jewish family enjoying a shabbat dinner (circa 1936)
Courtesy of myjewishlearning.com

Synagogue on Third Street (circa 1890)
Courtesy of California State Library

There are commonalities among the different branches or philosophies of Judaism. One of these is to achieve peace. Peace for Israel. Peace for the Jews in the United States. Peace so the holocaust would never happen again. Peace among community. Peace within the family. Peace within the Shul. Another of these is to comfort. The rabbis are professionally trained to provide comfort, but the community, the congregation, is equally equipped to offer comfort to those who struggle with losses and struggles.

This little book addresses several denominations within Judaism but attempts to show respect for all of them. To be reformed does not mean that you are less of a Jew than someone who is active in an Orthodox Temple. They just express their love for God within differing philosophies.

**Ruins of San Francisco Earthquake
with Synagogue in Background (circa 1907)
Courtesy of the California State Library**

**Temple Emanu-El in San Francisco (circa 1890)
Courtesy of the California State Library**

Hillel Jewish Scholarships Description

Temple Emanu-el San Francisco (circa 1890)
Courtesy of California State Library

Jews in Hollywood (circa 1942)
Courtesy of myjewishlearning.com

**Jewish children Decorating for Harvest Festival (circa 1962)
Courtesy of the University of California**

**Woman pickets to gain a Jewish divorce from her husband (circa 1954)
Courtesy of the University of California at Los Angeles**

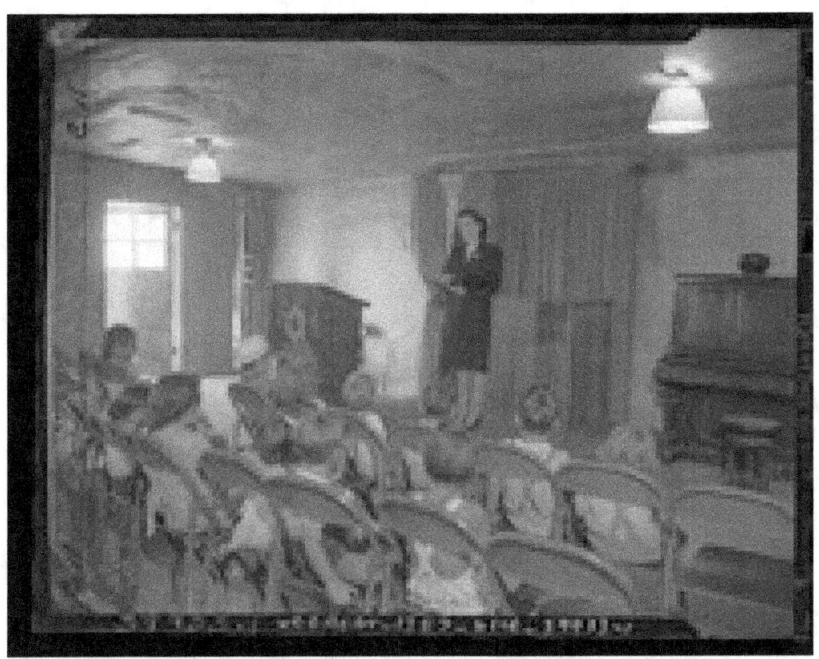

Jewish Sunday School Class (circa 1953)
Courtesy of the University of California Los Angeles

**Rabbi Moses J. Bergman Poster. Open the Gate of Palestine (circa 1947)
Courtesy of the University of California Los Angeles**

CHAPTER 2
CHASSIDIC

Men in long black coats walking through the fog. Bar-mitzvah boys pulled into afternoon/evening prayers. Visual strings from the ceremonial garment. Curled corner of the beard. The riches of community. Men with long gray beards walking through the fog.

Many Orthodox Jews participate in the Chabad House celebrations. Chabad House religious tenants are derived from the Chassidic tradition of Rabbi Lubavitch.

There are numerous Chabad houses in California. The Chassidic are orthodox Jews who observe the Old Testament and Talmud strictly. Each Chabad House represents a small Jewish neighborhood because typically members will live close enough to the Chabad House to be able to walk to it because observant Jews will not drive on the Sabbath because work is prohibited.

The author of this little book has experienced the joy of participation in Orthodox

Jewish Sabbath dinners and celebrations conducted in strict adherence to the

Old Testament laws. Each Chabad house is a community because the participants share the same zeal for God, hold to the same traditions and often dress in the same manner.

Chabad accepts any Jewish person whether both parents are Jewish, their mother is Jewish, their father is Jewish, they were raised Jewish or converted to Judaism. Chabad reaches out to the Jewish and non-Jewish community to help all people discover the greatness of God and to be a larger part of the local Jewish community

A typical Chabad house offers counseling, Rabbinic guidance, study groups, education on the history of Judaism and opportunities to share in the riches of Jewish life. Chabad offers counseling on drug abuse, alcohol abuse, sexual concerns, religious concerns, and family life. The Rabbinic guidance is often on how to know the Jewish laws, how to interpret them and how to follow them. The Orthodox Jewish Rabbi knows the Talmud and understands the traditional interpretations of the Old Testament law. The study groups can be of any size ranging from an intimate group of a few friends to dozens of people. Study group topics can include the Sabbath, Passover, Jewish architecture, career guidance, Torah, art, Jewish philosophy, how to become a Rabbi, how to become a Jewish social worker, the government of

Israel, the practice of Judaism in Israel and any other topic that would be of benefit to the attendees. Education on the history of Judaism can include the study of Abraham who was the first Jew, past generations and recent history such as the establishment of Israel. Opportunities to enjoy the riches of Jewish life include being part of Jewish neighborhoods, being part of Jewish communities, celebrating Jewish holidays, enjoying Jewish foods, and keeping a Jewish household.

Chabad has reached out to young people who are part of the counterculture. This includes bohemians, hippies, radicals and those who consider themselves out of the mainstream of life. Chabad is non-judgmental but instead accepts people as they are. Part of Chabad's purpose is to reach out to those who are disenfranchised, homeless, alcoholics, prostitutes, drug addicts, and persons that have been the victim of emotion, physical or sexual abuse. Chabad is equipped to reach out to these people serving as a social service agency in addition to be a religious one. Those that need this help and inspiration constitute a community which is a type of Jewish neighborhood.

Chabad will teach Jewish practices such as wearing tefillin which are straps and a headpiece with a box that contains Old Testament scripture in it. They will teach some basic practices of Judaism such as having one set of dishes for meat dishes and one for dairy dishes, attaching a mezuzah to the front door, wearing a yarmulke and wearing a tallis when in synagogue. Chabad teaches Jewish traditions such as touching the Torah when it is carried through the synagogue in a traditional manner. There is a traditional manner of dressing which for Jewish men are black pants, a white shirt and among many of the Chassidic a long black coat.

CHAPTER 3
SAN FRANCISCO

While San Francisco was an established town well before the discovery of gold in 1848. The Jewish population grew following the gold rush. If you gather a group of ten baby-boomers and observe their manner of dress, at least three are wearing Levi's. Many made fortunes mining gold, many just found specks, but all needed comfortable and rugged clothing able to withstand crossing streams and kneeling to operate gold mining equipment. Levi Strauss & Co. was founded in 1853 by Mr. Levi Strauss from Buttenheim Bavaria. The Golden Gate bridge that opened in 1937 was designed by Jewish Structural Engineer Joseph Strauss.

Theda Bara Jewish actress (circa 1922)
Courtesy of the California State Library

Union Square in San Francisco.
Temple Emanu-el in background (circa 1864)
Courtesy of the California State Library

Chapter Three

**Congregation Beth Israel on Geary near Fillmore (circa 1908)
Courtesy of the California State Library**

Jewish actress (circa 1912)

**Ruins of Jewish Temple Emanu-el in San Francisco (circa 1906)
Courtesy of the California State Library**

When my lovely wife, Patty, and I were first married we lived in the vicinity of Geary Street, Clement Street, Lake Street and 18th-26th Avenues which has multiple synagogues, and a Hebrew Day School. The Jewish community in Francisco is now developing in the Richmond District and Sunset Districts due to the recent immigration of Jews. In the late 1800s there were two small Jewish towns located in what is now referred to as the Richmond District.

Prior to the devastating earthquake in 1906 in the Jewish community of San Francisco was centered in the South of Market district.

There are no remnants of the Jewish Community that flourished there up until the 1906 earthquake. It now contains offbeat storefronts interspersed with micro condominiums. In the late 1840s small groups of Jewish people, mostly men, gathered to worship God and engage in Jewish practices.

The Eruv in San Francisco (circa 2017)
Courtesy of sfcurbed.com

Were they oppressed, did they have yarmulkes, did they have enough food, did they have a tallis, did they have tefillin, did they have Jewish books, did they have a Torah, did they have candles, did they have Jewish style foods to complete the end of the Yom Kippur fast. These questions are only answered by your speculations and your imagination. Try to transport yourself to 1849 and clarify your imagination to answer these queries. There was a Jewish mayor of San Francisco who served in that position from 1895-1897. That individual was Adolph Sutro who came from Prussia to engage in retail and wholesale business in the San Francisco Bay Area.

Congregation Sherith Israel in San Francisco

Multiple public libraries have numerous photos from the 1900s that depict Jewish life in the City. There was a large population of Eastern European Jews that populated what is now known as the South of Market region. After the 1906 earthquake many members of this neighborhood moved to the Fillmore neighborhood which was a vibrant and thriving Jewish neighborhood until the 1960s. A significant temple was Emanu-el which was used until 1925 until it was moved to its current location on Lake Street.

**Kairate Jews worshipping near San Francisco.
Courtesy of Karaite Jews of America**

Chapter Three

A Kairate Jew is one who believes that the Torah alone is enough to provide direction on conduct. This belief separates them from mainstream Judaism which accepts the Talmud as necessary to interpret the Torah.

A Paper titled the Marine Heritage Project written in the late 1800s described Judaism as it was found at that time. In the Project inspirational references to Judaism at that time in San Francisco were written., the contribution of Levi Strauss to Judaism in San Francisco was discussed. Jewish tradition and heritage helped separate the small population of Jews from the prevailing vices of violence, prostitution and other bawdy activity. The authors of the Paper described the elegance of Temple Sherith which reflects the architecture of Sephardic traditions.

The Jewish Community High School of the Bay (JCHS) inspires its students to learn, to be wise and to uphold Jewish values. Nancy Zimmerman Pechner and Noah Alper had a vision. A place where Jewish teenagers could learn in an encouraging and inspiring atmosphere. Their vision has been fulfilled. The school opened at Congregation Kol Shofar in Tiburon. JCHS started with 21 students in 2001. In 2002 the school moved to its permanent location in San Francisco. There are 19 classrooms, a performing arts center, art studio, music studio and an organic garden. The organic garden mimics the challenges of agriculture, viticulture, and forestry found in Israel today. The head of the school, Rabbi Howard Jacoby Ruben, is an attorney and graduate of Hebrew Union College.

The Brandeis School of San Francisco is a K-8 educational institution that instructs children in academics as well as Jewish values. Brandeis students want to improve the world rather than just feast on it for their own satisfaction. The low student to teacher ratio helps facilitate a nurturing environment. The parents of the students are encouraged to integrate into this welcoming environment. Do you think that students, teachers and families meet to enrich their lives long after students have graduated? I think so. Brandeis' mission includes kindness, integrity and service which guides students to success in the Jewish community and the secular world.

Bais Menachim Yeshiva Day School is an orthodox independent K-8 school that teaches students to succeed academically and to cherish the Jewish values of belief in God, a love for all, and acceptance for all. The school establishes a lush platform for community to thrive upon. Rabbi Yosef Langer, Chabad of San Francisco is the Head of the School.

Kehilla Jewish High School in Palo Alto is an independent Jewish college prep high school. The school's culture and community are enriched by their four principals which are; everyone counts, everyone has equal access to great learning, everyone's unique talents are valued equally, and we take responsibility for ourselves, our learning and our community.

Lisa Kampner Hebrew Academy was an orthodox Jewish day school. It is sad to see this school with about 50 students, close, but that is part of the often-shifting Jewish culture. It closed because school funding and leadership persons were both battling cancer and could not fulfill the roles that they once had. The school does continue their mission by offering educational programs for teens, and adults.

While the 1960s presented some negative practices and values, there were some neat things about the 1960s. One of these was the opportunity to express who you were or wanted to be. Much of this was occurring in the Fillmore District of San Francisco in the 1960s. (The authors email is oneoldhippie@ gmail.com). After the 1906 earthquake most of the Jewish people who were living in the South of Market district migrated to the Fillmore district. The Fillmore which remained a Jewish neighborhood until the 1960s or 1970s held many Jewish businesses, bakeries, markets, and synagogues. Many orthodox Jews lived in the Fillmore so they could walk to the synagogue on the sabbath. Orthodox Jews must not drive a car on shabbat because that is considered work. That mandate is followed today. We remember asking an orthodox Jew if he refrain from tearing toilet people on the sabbath because that work. He was so disappointed in us because we were missing the whole point of Judaism which is to rejoice in a living God.

Many Jewish young men and young women joined the counterculture, flower children or hippie movements. Some estimates are that 30 percent of the hippies were Jewish. There were many factors that contributed to this movement, but one was a rebellion against the strictness and austerity of the World War Two generation that stereotypically was harsh, regimented and severe. This is not to criticize that generation because they are still referred to as the Greatest Generation. The hippies rebelled. They wanted freedom. The hippie movement was intertwined with modern Jewishness.

Forsake the present and envision yourself in foggy San Francisco in the 1850s or 1860s. Did you have an Old Testament, was it in Hebrew or English, did you have any other Jewish books, did you have fragment of the Talmud, did you think that ownership of guns was acceptable for a Jew, did you carry a gun, did you wear a yarmulke, did you have a yarmulke, did you have a tallis? When there were consternations did the fog calm you?

What do you think of when you hear mention of Main County which is across the beloved Golden Gate Bridge from San Francisco? One might say wealthy, elitist. Although there are poor sections of Marin County most of it is upper middle class to upper class. There is a large population of Jewish people in Marin County. There are several synagogues, and a Jewish Community center. The Jewish Community Center, which is located in San Rafael, teaches about the life cycle including birth, childhood, bar mitzvah, adult bar mitzvah, parenting, living as a senior citizen and death. They are accepting of individuals converting to Judaism. The Jewish community in Marin County will allow a Gentile to convert to Judaism if they have a Jewish mentor, pass an interview asking why they choose Judaism, and have a mikvah bath.

Lighting the Menorah (circa 1972)
Courtesy of Thousand Oaks Library

**David's Jewish Restaurant in San Francisco (Circa 2017)
Courtesy of David's Delicatessen**

David's Jewish Restaurant in San Francisco (Circa 2017)
Courtesy of David's Delicatessen

**David's Jewish Restaurant in San Francisco (Circa 2017)
Courtesy of David's Delicatessen**

There are an estimated 70 synagogues in the greater San Francisco Bay Area. An example is Sherith Israel which is a reformed synagogue that has been in existence in different locations since 1851. Jessica Graf is the lead rabbi with David Frommer as the Cantor. This shul presents community, spirituality and knowledge. The sanctuary built in 1902 is in the classical revival and Romanesque Style. In 2012 the shul was added to the National Register of Historical Places.

Another well-loved synagogue in San Francisco is Congregation Beth Sholom which is located in the inner Richmond District. Beth Sholom is of the conservative tradition and reaches out to contemporary Jewish people. Even the building is modern which helps appeal to those who are chic. Dan Ain is the senior rabbi and Amanda Russel is the

Assistant Rabbi. Congregation Beth Israel Judea is a reformed synagogue with a hallmark of warmth, greeting and acceptance. A hello - a smile - a handshake - a simple greeting. These can lift a person's spirit more than illicit drugs or a therapist. What is an intimate gathering to you? Two, five, nine, seventeen. It depends on the person, but we all need to connect in personal and meaningful ways.

Congregation Chevra Thilim is an orthodox shul located in the Outer Richmond District of San Francisco. What is the appeal of Orthodoxy? Orthodox Jews, including Chassidic Jews constitute only about ten percent of the United State's Jewish population. In many ways it is harder to be an orthodox Jew than say a member of the reformed tradition. More rules to follow. What is the benefit? There is the benefit of working hard for your religion and being within the community that does so.

Berkeley, home to the academically prestigious University of California at Berkeley, has a healthy Jewish community largely connected to the University. There are several synagogues in Berkeley including Congregation Beth El, congregation Netivot Shalom, and congregation Beth Israel.

Hillel is a Jewish university system of organizations meant to meet the needs of Jewish college students. It was formed in 1923 and has a branch in Berkeley to serve the large population of Jewish people that study, work or teach at the University California at Berkeley.

Beth Israel is a Modern Orthodox synagogue with roots back to around 1915. It serves as a shul that seeks a strict and complete Jewish Experience but still adjust its adherence to Judaism to the current era. One description of Modern Orthodox Judaism is a movement within the orthodox culture that attempts to tailor Jewish Law and observance to the current culture that we are part of.

CHAPTER 4
SACRAMENTO AND STOCKTON AREA

Stockton's Temple Israel has one of the oldest Jewish populations in California. In the early 1850's several hundred Jewish people, primarily those who came to seek Gold during the gold rush that followed the discovery of gold in 1848, formed makeshift synagogues. This group of Jewish people formed Temple Israel, which is still happily in existing. There several Jewish businesses that formed in

Congregation B'Nai Israel in Sacramento (circa 2016)
Courtesy of thecompletepilgrim.com

Stockton during that time period. There are an estimated 15 synagogues located in the Stockton Sacramento area, most of them following the Reformed tradition. Reformed Jewry includes those who love being Jewish but do not follow the laws in the Torah strictly. Arden

Park in Sacramento has a large Jewish population and hosts many Jewish activities for the Jewish community to participate in. Arden Park is roughly the area surrounded by Fulton, Harley, Watt and Northrop avenues. There is an eruv in Sacramento which is used by the orthodox community. An eruv is a region in which an orthodox Jew can perform activities that are prohibited of the sabbath. In August 2008 an eruv was designated un the Arden-Arcade and Fair Oak neighborhoods which boasts a large population of Jewish people, many of whom are orthodox Jews. Parts of the eruv are designated using existing utility poles. An Eruv architect reviewed the Eruv to ensure that it followed orthodox tradition. The Jewish Federation of the Sacramento Region provides numerous services to the Jewish Community. These include services to Jewish families, scholarships, Jewish publications and senior programs. The Jewish people in the Sacramento region believe in God and the concept of the Messiah. Modesto hosts one synagogue which is of the conservative denomination. This serves as the Center of Judaism for greater Modesto and Stanislaus County. Modesto is remembered as the setting for the successful portrayal of the nostalgic teen culture of the 1950s and early 1960s. Modesto is also the subject of the author's title, "California's Highway 99: Modesto to Bakersfield. The Jewish population of Modesto and the Central Valley in the vicinity of Modesto is low but there still is one synagogue, Congregation Beth Shalom with Rabbi Shalom Bochner.

**Congregation Beth Shalom Courtesy of Diane N.
with Congregation Beth Shalom in Modesto**

Chapter Four

Yuba City is a small agricultural city about 60 miles north of Sacramento. There is one synagogue, which is part of the reformed tradition, in Yuba City/Marysville but there is no concentration of Jewish people that would constitute a Jewish neighborhood

Zofia Sokolowska, standing, showing her award
Center for Sacramento history

Numerous California cities have at least one synagogue and a noticeable Jewish population but would not necessarily be considered a Jewish neighborhood. Most are of the reformed tradition.

As an example, Redding does have a synagogue and an active Jewish community that is historical and current. The Jewish community in Redding as well as that in numerous small cities was established during the 1850s during the gold rush. We appreciate the initiative of a small group of Jewish women who gathered in Shingletown in 1975 to discuss the avenues that the Jewish community in that area would travel on. History does not tell us but were these women orthodox, conservative or reformed. Were they old or young. Did they have children with them. Was there one woman who was the organizer. Their charisma attracted other Jewish families to join them which led to the formation of the Redding Jewish Community center on Nov 10, 1976. This local center morphed into Congregation Beth Israel.

CHAPTER 5
OAKLAND AND THE REMAINDER OF THE SAN FRANCISCO BAY AREA

A significant part of Judaism in the greater San Francisco Bay Area is the Contra Costa Jewish Day School located in Contra Costa.

The Rohr Jewish Learning Institute teaches a course named "Worrier to Warrior": which focuses on achieving authenticity, embracing flaws, rethinking regret, peering through pain, living joyfully, and refreshing relationships.

Saul's Kosher style restaurant & delicatessen in Berkeley

The Author has lived in many places in the East Bay, particularly East Oakland. There is a funky, gentrified and upscale neighborhood, Lakeshore District, located east of Lake Merritt near downtown Oakland, which has a large Jewish population.

Temple Sanai in Oakland

West Oakland which was a low-income area in the early 1920s was a Jewish community complete with its own Jewish Community Center. In Oakland there were two kosher butchers. There are multiple synagogues in Oakland and the surrounding areas.

There are numerous book shops and gift shops in Oakland and the East Bay usually found within in a community center or synagogue. Los Gatos has a mikveh bath which is required after conversion to Judaism, after childbirth and at the end of a women's menstrual period. A contribution is customary, but certainly not required.

Reconstructionist Judaism was established by Mordecai Kaplan and seeks to integrate Jewish customs with modern scientific Judaism. There are about 10 reconstructionist synagogues in California. One concept that the Jewish people in Marin, as well as everyone in California, has in common is a love for Israel, which was reestablished in 1948. There is at least one reconstructionist synagogue in the Marin County area. This synagogue, which is similar to a reformed synagogue, attempts to integrate traditional beliefs and modern philosophies. Typically, Reconstructionist synagogues are somewhat different than the traditional Jewish denominations because they do not necessarily believe in the literal, personal, and ever-present God of Abraham, Isaac and Jacob that is described in the Tenach (Bible). Reconstructionist Judaism could easily be described as Liberal Judaism.

**Jewish delegates at the Biltmore Hotel (circa 1933)
Courtesy of the University of California at Los Angeles**

The City of San Jose hosts a large Jewish Community spread throughout the City and suburbs such as Santa Clara, Saratoga, Palo alto, Sunnyvale and Mountain View. There are over 15 synagogues, Jewish schools, and community centers, in this region. These range from reformed to orthodox. Reformed Judaism was formed early 1800s. At least one of the synagogues is conservative. The conservative movement began in the 1880s by Zachariah Franklin and Solomon Schlecter. Some posture that the conservative movement is in a state of decline with most Jews deciding to be Orthodox or adopt the tenets of the reformed Jewish tradition. Las Gatos which is an upscale suburb of San Jose contains a Jewish Community Center which is committed to meeting the need of the Jewish population. The center offers athletic activities, classes on family life and encouragement and recognition of the suffering of holocaust survivors. The participants in the Center love and support Israel which was reformed in 1948.

San Leandro, which is adjacent to Oakland contains Temple Beth Shalom, a conservative shul. Temple Beth Shalom is small but offers so many services, including Bar Mitzvah training, Sunday school, Shabbat services, weddings and counseling. It was formed in the 1940s primarily of San Leandro residents but many from adjoining communities attend the Shul. Temple Beth Shalom presents a warm and welcoming environment.

**Dr. Cyrus Adler discussing poor treatment of Jews in Germany (circa 1933)
Courtesy of the University of California at Los Angeles**

Reverence for the Torah (circa 1965)
Courtesy of the University of California at Los Angeles

Reading from the Torah. (circa 2011)
Courtesy of motherLodejewishcommunity.org

Periodically we learn of a Jewish congregation that is unaffiliated. They are not orthodox, conservative, reformed, reconstructionist, liberal or humanist. They are just Jewish people who want the intimacy and comradery found within the synagogue community. The Mother Lode Jewish Community (MLJC) is one of those. The Mother Lode area (Amador, Calaveras, Mariposa, and Tuolumne Counties) contains a very small Jewish population but in 1987 a few Jewish families formed the MLJC and it grew. In 1996 it was incorporated as a 501(c)3 non-profit corporation. They do not own a space, yet, but meet in local meeting rooms and restaurants. The holidays that they observe include Leil Selichot, the Jewish New Year, Day of Atonement, Feast of Tabernacles, Simchat Torah, Tu B'shvat, Passover, Purim and Lag B'omer.

Mishkon Tephilo Synagogue procession (circa 1948)
Courtesy of University of California at Los Angeles

The Magnes Collection of Jewish art and life is associated with the University of California at Berkeley. It contains 15,000 objects including images, from around the world. Professors, authors, scholars, students and the general public can access their collections. The Contemporary Jewish Museum is located in San Francisco in the Mission District and highlights the work of multiple Jewish artists.

**Newly elected President of B'nai B'rith (circa 1958)
Courtesy of the University of California at Los Angeles**

Temple Beth Abraham in Oakland is a conservative shul which was founded in 1907. Under the leadership of its Rabbi Mark S. Bloom who accepted the position of rabbi in 2001 Temple Beth Abraham has grown significantly adding 250 families to its membership. The synagogue offers sabbath prayers, bar-mitzvah training and rabbinic counseling. Temple Beth Abraham provides social services to those with various needs in the urban environment in which Temple Beth Abraham worships God.

Rabbi Harvey Block holding Torah (circa 1964)
Courtesy of the University of California at Los Angeles

Temple Beth Jacob in an orthodox shul also located in Oakland. At certain times in the Temple's history men and women sat together and at times woman and men sat on different sides of the sanctuary with a curtain separating the two. The reason for the separation is so the different genders would not be distracted by each other. Temple Beth Jacob has been attended by different Jewish populations, such as holocaust survivors who had a number tattooed on their arm. At the end of the main hallway there is a small chapel barely large enough for a minyan consisting of ten men. Rabbi Gershon, a graduate of Yeshiva University, is the senior rabbi at Temple Beth Jacob.

Oakland is home to Oakland Kosher Foods, established in 1962 which sells glatt kosher foods and serves a succulent selection of beef, lamb and poultry. This establishment has a collection of 800 bottles of kosher wine, the largest in Northern California. They operate under the strict supervision of Vaad Hakasrush.

Kehilla Community Synagogue, located in the exclusive enclave of Piedmont is a progressive, reconstructionist synagogue that encourages free expression, questioning the norm, and spiritual wellness. Kehilla participants may have a formal service and then the next day clean up a beach (Like we did in the late sixties and early seventies) Kehilla accepts everyone for who they are without judgement. Whether you are captain of the debating team or a hippie, an engineer or a bohemian, write contracts or write gentle poetry you are accepted at Kehilla.

CHAPTER 6
LOS ANGELES

Men in long black coats walking in the sunset. Bar-mitzvah boys pulled into afternoon/evening

prayers. Visual strings from the ceremonial garment. Curled corner of the beard. The riches of

community. Men with long gray beards walking in the muted sunset.

A bastion of sophistication, the elegance of the wealthy portions of Beverly Hills, the impoverished financially poor sections of Beverly Hills, successful screen actors and producers, Rodeo Drive, Watts, Glatt Kosher stores, ethnic diversity are all part of Los Angeles

The first known people in Los Angeles were the American Indians. The first know settler of Los Angeles was Juan Rodriguez Cabrillo 1542. Los Angeles was established and populated by Catholic Priests who established the missions. Los Angeles developed status as a city in 1835. Now there are four million people, about 600,000 Jewish, residing in Los Angeles. Many Jewish people are socially conscious and serve as a social benefit agency to Jews and Gentiles alike. These people serve as a benevolent organization in addition to be a religious one.

Los Angeles Jewish neighborhoods in the early part of the 20th century included the Temple Street area, and the Central Avenue area. These neighborhoods, located in downtown Los Angeles, were home to a large number of Jewish people, the Jewish population in these areas declined after 1925.

Anshe Ames located in the developing Pico-Robertson region of Los Angeles is an orthodox synagogue. The Shul on the Beach is an orthodox synagogue that draws members from the Venice Beach and surrounding areas. The Shul on the Beach emphasis the spirituality of Judaism and worships the omnipotent God. It has been a vibrant and welcoming enclave for several decades. There is a community that develops from the shul and from spending time together outside the Shul performing activities such as hiking or cycling. A yenta. A matchmaker. Arranged marriages. The Shul on the beach has a matchmaking service relying both on a database and in-person meetings at singles social events.

Solomon Finkelstein outside Breed Street Shul
Courtesy of the University of California at Los Angeles

Council of Jewish Women's Club (circa 1925)
Courtesy of the California State Library

In Los Angeles, as well as in the remainder of the California, is Yiddish still spoken at home? Yes, but there are not many who do. There are no published numbers because it is a concept that is hard to verify, but 1,000 people is the author's best determination. Is Yiddish a dying language – absolutely not. There are Jews in Israel that speak Yiddish. In ultraorthodox circles Children are taught Yiddish from birth and are taught to speak it at home. Yiddish is such a rich language. Why let it go. There are some passages in Yiddish that cannot be appropriately translated. Maybe we should learn it as a second or third language. Most people, Jew or Gentile, use Yiddish terms which they do not realize. The author's grandparents spoke Yiddish when they did not want their children and grandchildren to know what they were saying.

Jewish Youth examining Torah circa 1950
Courtesy of the University of California

Palm Springs is a hot but posh resort town about 50 miles east of Los Angeles. Do we remember that Sonny Bono of Sonny and Cher was the mayor of Palm Springs from 1988 -1994. It is permanently or temporarily populated by retirees or those in the entertainment community, many of whom are Jewish, looking for a less intense space in California. There is at least one shul (Jewish word for synagogue) in Palm Springs that offers high holiday services. Palm Springs does have a significant Jewish population as shown by the presence of eight Kosher restaurants, six Kosher hotels, two Jewish community organizations, one Jewish vacation rental, four synagogues, and one Mikvah. All of this for a City of 47,000 people! If you like Jewishness visit Palm Springs!

**Fox film corporation Jewish actress Bertha Kalich (circa 1922)
Courtesy of the California Public Library**

**German American Jewish Financial Leader
in San Francisco in the late 1800s (circa 1886)
Courtesy of the California State Library**

Chapter Six

Succoth customs (circa 1948)
Courtesy of the University of California at Los Angeles

**Nazimova, Jewish actress (circa 1921)
Courtesy of the California State library**

**Constructed as Jewish Temple
in Los Angeles in 1909. Now used as Church (circa 1971)
Courtesy of the California State Library**

UCLA Alan D. Leve Center for Jewish Studies

Some would say that Los Angeles and the millions of people living in the surrounding suburbs is a Jewish neighborhood but let us be a little more specific than that. As an aside what do we think of when we hear Anaheim? Disneyland, of course, a place that is indescribably enriching, which has at least 15 synagogues.

Dreyfus Wineky (circa 1885)

Jewish family in Beverly Hills (circa 1965)
Courtesy of UCL

Ben Dreyfus (circa 1880)

Chapter Six

**Jewish Life in the Fairfax District of Los Angeles
Courtesy of jpost.com**

The author has visited the Fairfax District several times in the past year when he was there on business. It is a Jewish neighborhood in decline. It was a vibrant and complete Jewish neighborhood that was once the center of Judaism in Los Angeles. The percentage of the Jewish population was so high that Los Angeles closed the schools in the area on Rosh Hashanah and Yom Kippur because the Jewish people were worshiping in the local synagogues. During Jewish festivals, events and holidays, portion of Fairfax avenue were closed. Only a few Jewish businesses populate the district now. A mural on a wall of Canters shows the history of the Jewish people in the Fairfax district. There is a remnant of Jewish people that live in the Fairfax district. These Jewish people live in integration with hipsters vising trendy streetwear shops.

**Groundbreaking for Temple Etz Chaim religious center.
Courtesy of Thousand Oaks Library**

Canters restaurant, an icon of the Fairfax District, opened in 1931. It truly is a family owned business operated by the third and fourth generations. Initially it was located in Boyle Heights, but when the Jewish population there decreased the Canter brothers opened the deli at its present location of 439 North Fairfax Avenue. Actually, this account all began in 1924 in Jersey City New Jersey. When the Stock market collapsed in 1929, the Canter brothers lost the deli, so they moved to California and opened Canter Brothers Delicatessen. The LA times said Canter's has the best pastrami. Celebrities, locals and tourists all visit Canter's. On the last few times that I visited Canters I have always had lox and bagel or the lox plate which gives you a little more lox, but next time I visit I will try the pastrami!

Let us now look at the Boyle Heights neighborhood, which was established as a Jewish enclave in the 1870s The author drove through Boyle heights in 2019 and could not find any remanants of the Jewish population that thrived there up until the 1960s or 1970s except for one, and it is a significant one – Breed Street Shul, or Congregation Talmud Torah.

This is an Orthodox Synagogue that was established in 1915 when there was a large immigrant Jewish population in the area. For several decades it was the largest orthodox synagogue in the United States. The Breed Street Shul was first constructed of wood framing. In 1923 a new synagogue was built out of unreinforced masonry. Because it is not reinforced with steel bars referred to as rebar the structure was more susceptible to damage in an earthquake. The los Angeles area has been the victim of many earthquakes but the Breed Street Shul was not damaged. As a licensed civil engineer, the author is able to professionally evaluate the condition of buildings and he did not observe any structural deficiencies at the Breed Street Shul. The synagogue is no longer in use and is now protected by a 6 feet high chain link fence with barbed wire. The synagogue ceased offering worship services in the 1980s when it was taken out of service because it did not local seismic retrofit requirements.

Breed Street Shul (circa 2017)
Courtesy of Los Angeles Department of City Planning

Next let us travel to Beverly Hills which is a short walk from the Fairfax district. Although portions of Beverly Hills are financially poor neighborhoods there is a large Jewish population living in Beverly Hills. Much of Beverly Hills is posh with professionals, actors, and producers living within its confines. There are two Chabad organizations in Beverly hills and there are several synagogues. It should be noted that there is a large group of Iranian Jews living in Beverly Hills.

We do not want to miss The Pico-Union Neighborhood which is funky and earthy. It has a multi-cultural art center with a Jewish presence. The neighborhood supports the Pico-Union Project which presents fun high holiday services.

Beverly wood is immediately adjacent to Beverly Hills. While not as prestigious it is still a desirable neighborhood. It does host a Chabad establishment. This Chabad offers services, parenting advice, and marital counseling. It hosts numerous Jewish documents and access to archived materials.

Pico-Robertson. A Glatt-Kosher supermarket. Wow! Let us first define what Glatt-Kosher means. Actually, we might want to define Kosher first. Kosher is defined as food that is fit for an observant Jew to eat. It includes excluding pork and shellfish from one's diet and other restrictions based on the Tenach and oral law. Now what does Glatt mean. It can mean that the lungs of an animal are smooth or more simply that the food is strictly kosher. There are sign after sign on markets and restaurants stating that the food is Glatt Kosher.

Sherman Oaks, in the San Fernando Valley, has the synagogue for the performing arts. While all are welcome at this synagogue unless we are in the entertainment industry we may feel out of place. This synagogue understands and caters to the stresses and joys associated with being a singer, dancer, producer or other occupation.

The La Brea district holds a large Orthodox Jewish community. There are many synagogues, Jewish shops and stores and yeshivahs. This is both an historic neighborhood as well as a developing one. There are both Chassidic Jews as well as Modern Jews residing in the La Brea District.

American Jewish University (AJU). AJU consists of two campuses, the Familian Campus located in Los Angeles and the Brandeis-Bardin Campus located in Brandeis which share one vision which is to enhance Jewish core values. Currently the Familian Campus is located in Belaire. The University was founded in 1947 as the University of Judaism, under the inspiration of Dr. Mordecai Kaplan. In 1941 the Brandeis Camp Institute was formed by Dr. Schlomo Badin to encourage young Jews to embrace the richness of Judaism. From its inception AJU was acknowledged for its teacher education and adult education programs. In 1979 an MA program in nonprofit management was added to the curriculum. A few years ago, the MA developed into an MBA program. AJU then developed a liberal arts program and a school of education. Initially the Brandeis Camp Institute was for young adults 18-26 but was eventually opened to adults of all ages. A large parcel of land owned by James Arness (Remember when we sat in the living room on Saturday nights and watched James Arness in Gunsmoke.) When the university of Judaism was combined with Brandeis-Bardin Institutes, American Jewish University was formed, to establish values such as the richness of Judaism, the viability of Judaism, and the importance of education. The inspiration and guidance of educational organizations such as AJI partially explain why so many Jewish young adults become business leaders, doctors, engineers, lawyers, teachers, civic leaders, accountants and members of other professions.

There are numerous Jewish Festivals in Los Angeles including: " Not that Jewish" offered by the Jewish Women's Theatre, Harvest Festival, Downtown Jewish History Tour, Jewish Boyle Heights-memories of Brooklyn Avenue, Jewish L.A. from Brooklyn Avenue to Fairfax Avenue, JNET Culver City Jewish Business Networking, the 2020 Jewish Executive Leadership Conference Los Angeles, High Holidays with the Jewish Collaborative of Orange County, and BHJC Rosh Hashana & Yom Kippur.

The Downtown Jewish History tour includes: Congregation B'nai Brith, which was formed in 1862, Congregation Beth Israel founded in 1899, Grand Central Market, Farmer's and Merchant's bank, Los Angeles Theatres on Broadway, and the Haas building.

The following images present the history of Congregation B'Nai Brith:

**Jewish explorer Solomon Karvahlo (circa 1890)
Courtesy of Wbla.org**

Joseph Newmark, a lay rabbi, and Rosa Newmark
Courtesy of Wbla.org

Rabbi Abraham Wolfe Edelman
Courtesy of Wbla.org

Chapter Six

Lighting the Menorah

Fort Street Temple (circa 1873)
Courtesy of the California State Library

Rabbi Emmanuel Schreiber, became rabbi in 1885
Courtesy of Wbla.org

**Rabbi Abraham Blum, became spiritual leader in 1889
Courtesy of Wbla.org**

**Rabbi Michael "Moses" G. Solomon
became rabbi in 1895 Wilshire Boulevard Synagogue
Courtesy of Wbla.org**

Synagogue at 9th and Hope
Courtesy of Wbla.org

Chapter Six

Wilshire Boulevard Temple (circa 1930)
Courtesy of the California State Library

Jews in North Hollywood gather around the Jewish bakeries that are opening in this area. The Jewish people in traditional garb stroll down Chandler Avenue. Outward appearance proceeds from inner holiness so the Jewish people in North Hollywood as well as in other Jewish enclaves fill their mind with thoughts of Torah, community and family. The traditional Chassidic and ultra-orthodox Jews reflect an inner prosperity. A Jewish neighborhood centers around the synagogue because orthodox

Jews cannot drive a car on the sabbath. The reason is that work is forbidden on sabbath, and lighting a fire is work and operating an internal combustion engine means that you are starting a fire. Thus, if there is one Orthodox Jewish Shul, there is a large Jewish population within easy walking distance of the Shul. There will also be glatt kosher bakeries, butcher's ad markets nearby. The number of synagogues in the past couple of decades has increased from one to our. The Jews in an orthodox neighborhood typically attend Jewish schools because it is very difficult to maintain Jewish observance to the Tenach (Torah, Writings and Prophets) in a secular environment. These schools range from permanent Jewish schools that can be quite expensive, to small schools meeting in people's living rooms. The education is religious and academic. The Eruv in this area is bordered the Venture Freeway, the San Diego Freeway, Sherman Way and the Bolden State Freeway. The Jewish population includes large populations of both Ashkenazi and Sephardic Jews. A mikvah was built which helps to complete the neighborhood. North Hollywood is now a complete Jewish community – not one that relies on Jewish services offered elsewhere in Los Angeles.

Each new Jewish neighborhood resists the declining Jewish population in the United States. Many decades ago, the percentage of Jews in the United States was four to six percent, but it is now down to about two percent of the population. Chassidic Jews are helping to reverse this trend by having large families. But what identifies a Jew. I think that most would agree that a child born to a couple with at least one parent Jewish. What if one parent is half Jewish and the other non-Jewish. Is that child Jewish? What about a child who was not born Jewish but somehow is raised Jewish - is that child Jewish? What about someone who converts to Judaism. Maybe we should expand the definition of Judaism, so the two percent does not become one percent.

Temple Beth Emut is in Burbank. Burbank is a city of 105,000 residents located north of los Angeles. It is an independent reformed temple with a rich heart. It is a close-knit group of families and single adults. They accept Jewish people wherever they are on their Jewish spiritual journey. Mark H. Sobel is the rabbi. Burbank Temple Emanu El hosts an elementary school which students and parents of students rave about. The Westside Jewish Community Center, located in Los Angeles, serves the Jewish residents of Burbank and surrounding cities. Each Jewish Community Center has a distinction or emphasis. This JCC emphasizes wellness, encouragement to meet the needs of people with special needs, senior fitness, adult fitness and community supported agriculture. Community Supported Agricultural. Terms that come to mind are community garden, organic garden, vegetarian and vegan. A community garden teaches participants many things including peace, calmness, and a oneness with others who tend and till the soil in the garden.

The Pasadena Jewish Temple and Center, located in Altadena, a conservative Shul is a center of Jewish life in the city. The temple opened in 1920.

Kosherica, a glatt kosher, modern Jewish resort of offers Kosher Cruises and Passover celebrations. Varied and desirable location that one can cruise to include the Caribbean, Alaska, the Mediterranean, Ireland, South America, and Baltic/Russia. There is a Jewish music festival at sea cruise also serving glatt kosher food.

To explore your own family's history, consult the Jewish Genealogical Society of Los Angeles. The JGSLA was founded in 1979 and is governed by an elected Board of Directors. Among its many services is offering assistance to those wishing to research their own family's history such as where our relatives were born who they were married to and the children that they had. They have taught computer skills to be used in performing research, histories of individuals and relevant publications.

Los Angeles is home to an estimated 25 Jewish Schools ranging from those who offer prekindergarten, kindergarten, K-8 and K-12. These range from those that have only a scent of Judaism to those that are strictly orthodox with an emphasis on the Torah and Talmud. One of these many schools is TVT Community Day School which has over 600 students and provides educational services to pre-kindergarten to 12th grade children. Milken Community Schools is a grade 7-12 school with a 7:1 student teacher ratio with over 800 students enrolled there. Why a Jewish School? There are secular charter schools, other private schools and some very good public schools. One reason why Jewish parents seek out, often expensive Jewish education, is because the richness of Judaism flows into the academic environment. Sure the students are there to learn academics that will help them succeed in college or other paths of lire, but they are also there to learn the love of Israel, love of the Torah, and to love other Jewish people, to love all of the people on the planet and to change things for the benefit of humanity.

Yavneh Hebrew Academy teaches both excellent academic skills but also a love for Judaism. Yavneh Hebrew Academy seeks to instill confidence in students so they will believe the best about themselves, develop ways to be successful within their own individual talents, abilities and environmental experiences. To enhance what the school can teach them parents, siblings and extended family are invited to be part of the community. This parental involvement shows in a tangible way how much a child's parents care about them. Yavneh adopt the four Cs which are critical thinking, collaboration, creativity and communication. In addition to this, Yavneh Hebrew Academy has their own acronym with is RISE (Rigor, innovation, creativity and communication).

There are other Jewish schools in the Los Angeles area including the Bais Yaakov School for Girls and the Ginda Maimonides Academy. The Ginda Maimonides Academy presents numerous Core Values. These include excellence, drive, responsibility, passion, connection, respect, and commitment. Passion for what: Mitzvot, being kind to other people, the Torah, protecting the planet on which we live, family, community and Almighty God. Their new 50,000 sf facility serves as an origination center. Engineering and science are the core activities performed in this building. What will these children accomplish at this young age or as adults: Cures for diseases, educational techniques, advancement of our political system. One of Ginsa Maimonides goals is to prepare students to do major and significant things as they progress through life. The school is credentialed by the California Association of Independent Schools (CAIS).

Hancock Park located in central Los Angeles is a developing Chassidic Jewish neighborhood. Most of the major segments of orthodox Judaism including Chassidic Jews are represented in this neighborhood. Other Jewish neighborhoods include Mid-Wilshire, Silver Lake, Echo Park and the Miracle Mile. The Mid-Wilshire neighborhood is home to many Jewish service organizations. Other Jewish population include Encino, Sherman Oaks, Tarzana and Studio City.

The Jewish population of the Los Angels Metropolitan Area hosts approximately 600,000 Jews. That is roughly 15% of the population of the Los Angeles metropolitan area. These include orthodox, conservative, reformed, reconstructionist, humanistic, independent, modern orthodox, Jewish renewal, Sephardic and traditional.

There are about 250 Jewish synagogues in the Los Angeles Metropolitan area. Many of these ae located in the San Fernando Valley. Encino/Tarzana has a significant Jewish population of an estimated 3,000-5,000 Jewish people in that area. There were many entertainment company owners such as Harry Warner, Albert Warner, Louis Mayer, and Samuel Goldwyn that populated the Hollywood region of Los Angeles.

The center of a small town is city hall, a restaurant and a small general store, but the center of a Jewish neighborhood is the kosher butcher. There are an estimated twenty-five kosher butchers in the Los Angeles greater area. Examples are Rabbi's Daughter, Beverly Hills Kosher Meat Market, and Western Kosher Pico branch, and Western Kosher Fairfax Branch. Keeping the Old Testament Laws is important enough to pay the significantly higher price of Kosher meat which is due to the costs of inspection and certification. Twenty-five Kosher Butchers in the LA area is quite a few compared to the San Francisco Area which has about four.

CHAPTER 7
LONG BEACH,
SAN DIEGO THE CENTRAL VALLEY

The Jewish community in Long beach developed late as compared to other communities. The first Jewish person arrived around 1900. By about 1915 the community was about 50 people. Many of the Jewish men opened businesses in the produce market. Currently there about 20,000 Jews in Long beach and the surrounding areas.

Jewish Community Center
Courtesy City of Long Beach

Hanukkah Celebration
Courtesy City of Long Beach

MALIBU JEWISH CENTER & SYNAGOGUE

Courtesy of mjcs.org

The Malibu Jewish Center and Synagogue located in Malibu is a reconstructionist synagogue which is considered a liberal Jewish organization. The Malibu Jewish Center is led by Rabbi Michael Schwartz who has an extensive resume of involvement with and leadership of Jewish organizations. Malibu is considered a Jewish neighborhood because of the high percentage of the residents being Jewish.

The first Jew arrived in San Diego and lived in Old Town in 1850. Roughly 30 Jews lived in San Diego until around 1870. Shortly after that the Jewish population moved to the San Diego Bay area. By the 1950s this neighborhood had established itself as a Jewish Center, with Jewish shops and reformed, conservative and orthodox synagogues. The Jewish population of San Diego is unique in that it includes a significant number of Jews from Mexico. Much of the Jewish community of San Diego is organized under the Jewish Federation of San Diego County. This organization supports youth and seniors. It provides chaplaincy services. It takes actions to support the Nation of Israel.

San Diego Chabad hosts a resort in San Diego that is close enough to Chabad of Pacific Beach that it is within walking distance of beaches. Totally Jewish Travel sponsors resort like activities at the Hilton De Mar Hotel in San Diego. The actives at the hotel include the 10-day Passover celebration for all Jewish philosophies including orthodox, conservative, reform, Chassidic, ultra-orthodox and liberal. This celebration offers luxurious dining experiences, great sermons from professional Jewish speakers, family social gatherings and fun entertainment. There are choices of setting for celebrating the Passover; including a group Seder led by a rabbi, a semi-private Seder with a small group or a separate room just for your family. The onsite rabbi ensures that the good is Glatt Kosher. What a way to celebrate Pesach!

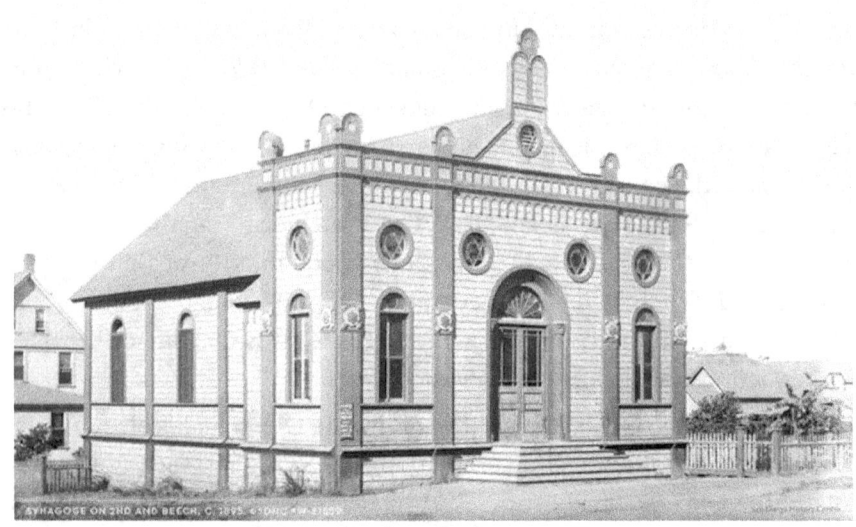

**Synagogue at 2nd and Beech in San Diego
Courtesy of San Diego History Center**

The synagogue appears to be built with wood framing and wood siding on a concrete foundation. Note that there is an oversized front which was typical of western architecture of that time.

March in Support of Israel (circa 1973)
Courtesy of San Diego History Center

1958 photo of Passover Celebration
Courtesy of San Diego History Center

Isidor Lewis Cigars (circa 1895)
Courtesy of San Diego History Center

The southern Central Valley, which is a largely agricultural area does not contain many Jewish people. There are however small pockets of Jewish people currently living these and quite a lot of history of the Jews that migrated to America from Germany. One example is Mr. David Hirschfeld who was a Jewish merchant in the 1890s. David came to the United States in 1871. As a young adult he joined Hirschfeld Brothers and Company. Then, showing initiative and courage, he opened the Pioneer Store. There were many other Jewish Pioneers in the Bakersfield area including the Hoch Heimer Family, Henry Jastro who was a civic leader in Bakersfield, and Alphonse & Henrietta Weill. Moses and Lena Lewinsky Brum were prominent Jewish leaders and merchants in the Gold Rush towns. Barstow, we envision a place that is hot, rural, small and could not have much of a Jewish Community. Well maybe that is not so. They have a conservative Jewish Shul in town, Synagogue Baridhara Shel

Haram. So, there is enough of a Jewish population in Barstow to support a shul!

Does the dramatic and lush Yosemite National Park where people live, and visit have a Jewish population? Yes, they do! Camp Towanna. This Jewish rustic camp which is located within eight miles of Yosemite National Park. Camp Towanga was established in 1925 to help young men and young ladies have a positive self-image, a spiritual approach to life, a belief in God and to establish community among the campers and the Northern California Jewish Community. In addition to Camp Towanga. There is even a Jewish Park Ranger in Yosemite National Park, Scott Gediman. The Awhanee Hotel in Yosemite Valley hosts several Jewish weddings a year. Of the four million US citizens and those from around the world that visit the park an estimated 50,000 Jewish people visit the park each year.

What about Alturas – does that teeny tiny town in the northeast corner of California have a Jewish history? In 1848 Emmanuel Lauer came to the United States from Bavaria. He moved to Alturas in 1872 and opened several businesses including The Bank of Modoc County. Today the closest synagogue is in Klamath Falls, Oregon, Shalom Temple Ministries, which serves the Jewish people who live at the northernmost areas of California.

Chapter 8
Conclusion

If you would like your organization to be referenced in any future printings of the book, please feel free to send pictures and a textual description. Keith Warwick, PE welcomes your comments, questions and discussion. You can be given credit in the caption line if you would like to be.

BIBLIOGRAPHY

1. Chabad
2. Jewish in San Francisco
3. Jewish in Stockton
4. Jewish in San Francisco
5. Jewish Museum of the American West
6. My Jewish Learning
7. SF Curbed
8. Karaite Jews of San Francisco
9. Marine Heritage Project
10. The Jewish Traveler

INDEX

Boyle Heights	57
Chassidic	11
Dreyfus winery	52
Fairfax district	55
Fox Film	47
Los Angeles	43, 44, 45, 46, 47
Mother Lode	38
Oakland	33, 39, 41
Pico Robertson	59
Redding	31, 32
San Francisco	13
San Leandro	36
Saul's	33
Sherman Oaks	59
UCLA	52
West Oakland	34
Wilshire Blvd. Shul	67

www.ingramcontent.com/pod-product-compliance
Lightning Source LLC
Chambersburg PA
CBHW071851230426
43671CB00012B/2147